The Arizona Book!

**The Things You'll See!
The Places You'll Go!**

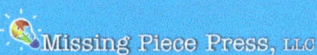

The Arizona Book
Copyright © 2020 Kevin J. Brougher & Lisa Santa Cruz

ISBN# 978-0-9977959-8-1
Library of Congress Control Number : 2019919324

All rights reserved.
No part of this book may be reproduced by any means
without the written permission of the publisher.
Printed in U.S.A.

Distributed in United States and Canada by Allied Resources - Abilene Texas.
For wholesale and licensing inquiries, please email
us at : Questions@MissingPiecePress.com

Missing Piece Press, LLC does not accept unsolicited manuscripts.
Visit : MissingPiecePress.com for information on our other fun products.
LIKE us on Facebook to keep up to date with our new books, games and special offers.
"A little Thinking...a LOT of FUN!" is a trademark of Missing Piece Press, LLC.

Other Publications from Missing Piece Press

Thinklers! 1 : A Collection of Brain Ticklers!
Thinklers! 2 : More Brain Ticklers!
Thinklers! 3 : Even More Brain Ticklers!
Thinklers! 4 : Full-Color Brain Ticklers!
History Mysteries : A New Twist on Time-Lines
State Debate : 50 Unique Playing Cards and 50 Games
Number Wonders : A Collection of Amazing Number Facts!
Dreams, Screams, & JellyBeans! : Poems for All Ages
The Storybook : A novel for ages 10 on up
Science Stumpers : Brain-Busting Scenarios...Solved with Science
Algebra Summary Sheets : Posters to Promote Proficiency
Reindolphins : A Christmas Tale
Who Says Hoo? : A Book for Babies & Toddlers
Grandpa Kevin's... ABC Book : Really Kinda Strange...
Grandpa Kevin's...Book of COLOR : Really Kinda Strange...
Number Fun! : A Book of Counting and Numbers for Toddlers
Who's Waiting for You? : A Book of Animal Clues for Toddlers

Frazzle : A Frenzied Game of Words
ShanJari : An African Game of Sequence and Strategy
Whew! : Words, Wits, Whims & Woes!
TooT! : A Nerdy Little Game
Blam! : A Different Card Game
DICE Blam! : A Different Dice Game
Word Nerd : A Quick-Witted Word Game
Bunco BUDDIES! : The BETTER Bunco Game
Take Twelve : The Token Taking Game
CRUMMY : The Criss-Cross Rummy Game
Round About : A Little Thinking - A LOT of FUN!
Whole Enchilada : It All Adds up to FUN!
Besto : An Animal Matching Game
Fifty Nifty : United States Playing Cards & Games
The Get-to-Know-You Game : Fun for Families & Friends

A Little Thinking...a LOT of FUN! ™

Missing Piece Press, LLC
MissingPiecePress.com

Copyright © 2019 Missing Piece Press, LLC

This is by no means a complete list of all the amazing places to go and things to see in Arizona. But, if you are a visitor for a week or planning on staying for years, this book if a fun way to record the fantastic places, plants and animals that you will undoubtedly encounter.

ARIZONA BIRDS

Roadrunner

- This bird never needs to drink.
- Their diet can include spiders, lizards, scorpions and rattlesnakes.
- They can reach a running speed of 20 mph.

☐ I've seen it!

Cactus Wren

- It is the state bird of Arizona.
- It nests in cactus plants for protection.
- It is the largest wren species in North America.

☐ I've seen it!

Cardinal

- It is the state bird of seven states.
- Both male and female sing, though the female usually sings longer and more complex songs.
- They are non-migratory.
- The male can spend long hours fighting his reflection in a window.

☐ I've seen it!

Raven

- These birds are one of the smartest animals.
- They are playful.
- They use hand gestures.

☐ I've seen it!

Great Horned Owl

- They can turn their heads 270 degrees.
- Their crushing power is around 300 psi.
- They can have a wingspan up to 60 inches.

☐ I've seen it!

Arizona Verdin

- Although it resembles members of the chickadee family, it is the only bird in the genus Auriparus.
- Their roosting nests help them stay warm in winter. These nests have thick insulation and may reduce the energy required to stay warm by as much as 50%.
- One pair in Arizona was observed building 11 nests in one year.

☐ I've seen it!

Turkey Vulture

- These birds are scavengers and feed primarily on decaying flesh.

- These birds lack the powerful feet that are characteristic of other raptors like eagles and hawks. They have long toes with blunted talons, which help ithem to walk.

- They lack a voice box; their vocalizations include rasping hisses and grunts.

 I've seen it!

Quail

- Certain species of this bird have a plume (also known as topknot), shaped like a teardrop, on top of the head. It bobs as they walk.

- These birds are able to fly short distances, but they spend most of their time on the ground.

- They are part of the pheasant family.

 I've seen it!

Harris Hawk

- This hawk has a wingspan of about 3.6 feet.
- As in other raptors, females are 35% larger as compared to males.
- Yellow legs and brown plumage are the two basic physical characteristics.

 I've seen it!

Gila Woodpecker

- These birds tend to bang loudly on metal chimneys and pipes to announce their territories and also to attract mates.
- This woodpecker builds its home wherever it is possible. Though it prefers to build houses in saguaro cacti.
- This species of woodpecker is noisy and blaring.

 I've seen it!

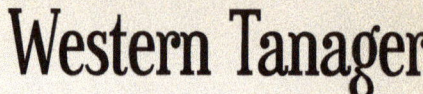

Western Tanager

- This bird's red face is acquired through it's diet of insects.
- The species was first recorded on the Lewis and Clark expedition.
- A group of them is called a "Season".

☐ I've seen it!

Morning Dove

- They are also called "Turtle Doves".
- Egg incubation takes just two weeks.
- They have been clocked at 55 mph.

☐ I've seen it!

Hummingbird

- At least 13 species have been seen in Arizona.
- The most common in Arizona is the Anna's species.
- These birds prefer a solitary life.

☐ I've seen it!

Southwestern Towhee

- This bird is a type of large sparrow that belongs to the family of buntings.
- This bird uses morning dew from leafy vegetation to wash itself.
- They produce a rattling song that consists of repeating phrases.

☐ I've seen it!

Gray Hawk

- This smallish raptor is also known as the Mexican Goshawk.

- They feed mainly on lizards and snakes but, will also eat small mammals, birds and frogs.

- These hawks were common in Arizona in the late 1800s, but habitat degradation, particularly the clearing of mesquite and cottonwood forests along streams saw a decrease in their numbers.

☐ I've seen it!

ARIZONA MAMMALS

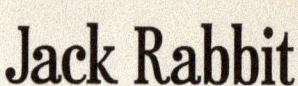

Jack Rabbit

- These speedy animals are capable of reaching 40 mph and leaping 10 feet.
- The young mature quickly and require little care from their mothers.
- They like to eat grass, bark, roots, twigs, and leaves. They even eat prickly pear cactus and desert shrubs!

 I've seen it!

Bobcat

- These mammals are found only in North America.
- They often ambush their prey by waiting motionless and then pouncing on them.
- They will usually change their shelter on a daily basis.

☐ I've seen it!

Coyote

- They are often mistaken for small to medium sized domestic dogs.
- They vary their diet with the seasons. Cactus fruit, mesquite beans, flowers, insects, rodents, lizards, rabbits, birds and snakes make up some of their dietary choices.
- Coyotes have a central den site which is used for rearing their pups and sleeping.

☐ I've seen it!

Javelina

- These live in large family groups. The average group size is 10 or less, but a few herds have known to number up to 53 animals.
- They are also known as the Collared Peccary.
- They have a scent gland on the top of their rump covered by long hairs. They will rub their scent on rocks and tree stumps to mark their territory, as well as rubbing the scent on each other to help with identification.

☐ I've seen it!

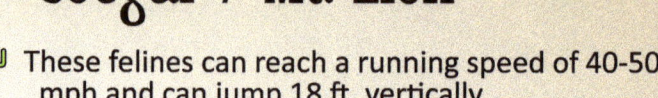

Cougar / Mt. Lion

- These felines can reach a running speed of 40-50 mph and can jump 18 ft. vertically.
- They are more closely related to a house cat than a lion.
- There is a difference in the structure of their voice box or the larynx so, instead of roaring like a lion, they produce a high pitched scream.

☐ I've seen it!

Pack Rat

- These mammals often settle their nests under the hoods of cars, in large piles of wood or garbage, and even in attics and cacti.
- They are particularly fond of shiny objects.
- These rodents are nest builders. They use plant material such as twigs, sticks, and other available debris.

☐ I've seen it!

Wild Burrows

- This mammal was first introduced into the Southwest desert by Spaniards in the 1500s.
- These pack animals are sure-footed, can locate food in barren terrain and can carry heavy burdens for days through hot, dry environments.
- Although some moisture is provided by plant material, wild burros must have drinking water throughout the year.

☐ I've seen it!

Round-Tailed Squirrel

- Usually found in trees, this desert variety are ground dwellers.
- They resemble a tiny prairie dog and share some of its habits.
- They often stand on their hind legs trying to get a better view as they watch for their many predators.

☐ I've seen it!

Wild Horses

- These mammals in southern Arizona, lacking ample prairie grass, nibble on tree leaves and other plants.
- Coyotes and mountain lions are among their largest desert predators; however they pose a minimal threat.
- It is believed that they arrived in the southwest with Spanish explorers in the 1600s and with miners in the 1800s.

☐ I've seen it!

Longhorn Antelope

- The horn (not antler) is shed, which is unlike any other animal.
- This high-strung animal is active night and day.
- These animals cannot leap fences, like deer can, so fenced rangeland has hampered their migration.

☐ I've seen it!

Coatimundi

- This mammal is related to the racoon.
- They sleep in trees and prefer elevations of 4,500 to 7,500 ft., but they occasionally travel to lower deserts in the winter.
- They are social creatures. Females and their young travel in groups of as many as 30 individuals for protection from mountain lions.

☐ I've seen it!

Black-Tailed Prairie Dog

- These rodents live in groups to help protect themselves from predators.
- They do not need a source for water.
- They use an extensive system of vocalizations to communicate with the rest of the colony.

☐ I've seen it!

Wild Desert Cottontail

- These mammals are named after their tail.
- They are coprophagic, meaning they eat their own feces.
- When alarmed, they can run up to twenty mph in a zigzag pattern.

☐ I've seen it!

Black Bear

- It is the only species of bear still found in Arizona.
- An average male will weigh from about 115 to 600 pounds and females weigh between 90 and 400 pounds.
- Typically, they are solitary animals except in family groups of mother and cubs, breeding pairs or when they congregate at feeding sites.

☐ I've seen it!

Mexican Gray Wolf

- This is the smallest subspecies of this canine mammal.
- It mainly feeds on small animals like squirrels and mice.
- It also goes by the name "Lobo".

☐ I've seen it!

Desert Badger

- These mammals are part of the weasel family and can become ferocious.
- They are carnivorous and mostly nocturnal.
- They dig into burrows with long claws and eat ground squirrels, prairie dogs, gophers, snakes and lizards.

☐ I've seen it!

Mule Deer

- They gained their name from their large mule like ears.
- These deer have a 310 degree view around themselves because of the position of their eyes on the sides of their heads.
- Compared to the white-tailed deer, they are bulkier, have larger ears, a black-tipped tail, a whiter face, are a third larger, and have bigger antlers that fork out instead of branch from a single shaft.

☐ I've seen it!

Western Pipistrelle Bat

- This is the smallest bat in the United States.
- They are among the first bats to emerge in the evening.
- They hibernate in mines, caves and rock crevices.

☐ I've seen it!

ARIZONA PLANTS

Yucca

- Unlike most agaves, most of these are polycarpic (blooming more than once).
- About 10 species occur in the Sonoran Desert region.
- With only one exception, reproduction depends on moths which deliberately cross-pollinate the flowers.

☐ I've seen it!

Mexican Bird of Paradise

- If frosts never occur, this flowering plant can grow 15 to 25 ft. tall and 12 to 18 ft. wide.
- Their large bright flowers provide vibrant color for long periods of time.
- The shades of yellow, fiery red and orange contrast with the feathery foliage.

☐ I've seen it!

Palo Verde

- The name is Spanish and means "green stick".
- It's the Arizona State Tree!
- They can easily live a century.

 I've seen it!

Mesquite Tree (flowering)

- This plant is a hardy desert tree that has adapted over centuries to live in desert landscapes.
- The Mesquite tree's lateral roots can reach out much further than the canopy. They also have tap roots that go very deep to get water - sometimes as deep as 150 ft. down, however, 50 ft. down is more typical.
- The beans from the mesquite tree are nutritious, sweet and protein rich.

 I've seen it!

Mistletoe

- This plant is a parasite that steals water and nutrients from other plants.
- There are about a dozen species of this plant in the southwest.
- Birds carry the berries to other plants where they can sprout and grow.

 I've seen it!

Cholla (Staghorn)

- This cactus has forked branches that resemble deer antlers.
- It can be shrubby or treelike and can grow up to 15 feet tall.
- The fruit is fleshy and usually doesn't have spines (thorns) and the fruit stays on the cactus for a year before falling off.

 I've seen it!

Creosote Bush

- This plant, also called "Greasewood", is a large shrub found in most of Arizona's counties.
- When wet, the foliage creates the signature smell of a desert rain.
- This bush has also been used by indigenous people for the treatment of at least fourteen afflictions and diseases.

☐ I've seen it!

Aloe Vera

- These succulent plants are hardy and long-lived. Wild species have been known to survive for 100 years.
- There are approximately 250 species of this plant but only 4 of them are cultivated for their health benefits.
- The most valuable part of the plant is the clear gel found inside the leaves, which contains 75 health-giving nutrients, including amino acids, vitamins, minerals and enzymes.

☐ I've seen it!

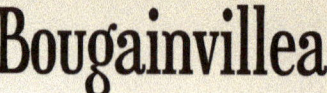

Bougainvillea

- Bougainvilleas are tropical plants that thrive in outdoor areas with low rainfall and intense heat.
- In tropical places, they can bloom all year round.
- The vine species grow anywhere from 3 to 40 ft. tall, scrambling over other plants with their spiky thorns.

☐ I've seen it!

Blooming Cactus

- Some of these flowers bloom for only a day, while others can last for weeks.
- Many of these flowers are nocturnal, meaning they bloom only at night.
- These flowers are usually pollinated by bees, butterflies, moths and even bats.

☐ I've seen it!

Organ Pipe Cactus

- This cactus' habitat is rocky, sandy and generally inhospitable and unfertile ground.
- The cactus is the second largest in the U.S. (next to the Saguaro) growing as tall as 23 feet.
- The fruit has provided a food source to Native Americans for centuries.

☐ I've seen it!

Blooming Agave

- These plants are monocarpic, meaning they die after they sprout a large stalk.
- The plant has the common name "Century Plant" because it supposedly takes a century for the stalk to sprout.
- When this happens, the stalk resembles an asparagus spear.

☐ I've seen it!

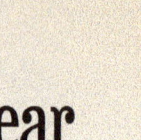

Prickly Pear

- This name of cactus represent about a dozen species of the Opuntia genus.
- All have flat, fleshy pads that look like large leaves.
- The fruits of most of the species are edible and sold in stores under the name "Tuna". The branches, or pads, are also cooked and eaten as a vegetable.

☐ I've seen it!

Ocotillo

- This is one of easiest plants to identify in the desert.
- It is named after the cluster of fiery red flowers you can find at the end of their stems from about March to June.
- When the water dries up, the leaves will fall and the plant will rely on the chlorophyll inside its stems to photosynthesize.

☐ I've seen it!

Agave

- It's nickname is the "Century Plant".
- Most species are essentially stemless but a few grow trunks that creep along the ground. Many sprout once - then die.
- Various species have also been important sources of food, fences, rope, medicine and liquor.

☐ I've seen it!

Barrel Cactus

- They usually grow along desert washes, gravely slopes and beneath desert canyon walls in hot dry climates.
- In an emergency, the pulp of the stem can be chewed for its food and water content.
- Native Americans boiled young flowers in water to eat like cabbage and mashed older boiled flowers for a drink.

☐ I've seen it!

Teddy Bear Cholla

- This cactus relies on detached segments to form new plants by rooting and growing. It produces no seed.
- It can be distinguished by its dense, straw-colored spines and yellow to green flowers.
- A myth is that it "jumps" out at a passerby.

 I've seen it!

Yellow Brittlebush

- The branches of this bush are brittle and woody and contain a fragrant resin.
- In the late winter and early spring small yellow flowers form on long stalks well above the leafy stems.
- This plant is a member of the Sunflower family.

 I've seen it!

Saguaro

- When rain is plentiful and the cactus is fully hydrated it can weigh between 3,200–4,800 pounds.
- The Sonoran Desert is the only place in the world where you can find this cactus.
- The Carnegie Institution funded the formation of the Desert Botanical Laboratory in Tucson in 1903, and in Carnegie's honor the scientific name of the cactus was dubbed "Carnegiea Gigantic".

I've seen it!

ARIZONA REPTILES

Coachwhip (Red Racer)

- This reptile eats a wide variety of animals including lizards, snakes (including rattlesnakes), mice, birds, insects, bats, frogs, toads and small turtles.
- It is one of the largest snake species found in North America.
- In Arizona there are three subspecies: Sonoran Coachwhip, Lined Coachwhip and the Red Racer.

☐ I've seen it!

Desert Tortoise

- Water is stored in the bladder of this reptile and they can survive 1 year without water.
- Young ones are light colored whereas the adult animals are usually dark colored.
- They dig burrows in the soil for survival and spend 95% of their life there.

☐ I've seen it!

Spiny Lizard

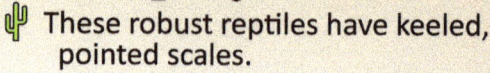

- These robust reptiles have keeled, pointed scales.
- These lizards exhibit metachromatism, which is color change as a function of temperature. When it is cooler, colors are much darker.
- Males have two large, bright, blue-green patches on the belly and a blue-green patch on the throat.

☐ I've seen it!

Horned Lizard

- When threatened these reptiles will inflate their bodies and hiss.
- Some species can even shoot a stream of blood from the corners of their eyes.
- They must bask in the sun to reach a specific body temperature before foraging for food with their fast sticky tongues.

☐ I've seen it!

Rattlesnake

- Scientists have identified 36 species of this reptile - 13 of which live in Arizona - more than any other state.

- They use the "loreal pit," a heat-sensing organ between the nostril and eye to locate prey.

- They have glands that make venom, much like human saliva glands make saliva but, less than 1% of this snake's bite result in human deaths.

 I've seen it!

California King Snake

- They are highly tolerant of and perhaps immune to a rattlesnake's venom and will sometimes begin consuming the rattlesnake before it is dead.

- When confronted, this reptile can release a foul-smelling musk.

- There are 10 species and 45 subspecies of this ground-dwelling non-venomous snake.

 I've seen it!

Sonoran Mt. Snake

- This reptile has alternating red, black and white bands.
- In Arizona this snake is found at elevations ranging from 3,000 ft. to 9,000 ft.
- When captured this snake does not hesitate to bite and discharge foul-smelling musk and feces.

☐ I've seen it!

Southwestern Speckled Rattlesnake

- This particular rattlesnake has salt-and-pepper speckles over its back.
- Northwestern Arizona specimens are often pink or peach.
- They are capable of delivering large amounts of potent venom.

☐ I've seen it!

Sonoran Ground Snake

- Base color of this reptile can be light tan, cream, gray, blue-gray, or orange-red and has many pattern variations.
- This harmless snake is commonly encountered in yards in the Phoenix metropolitan area.
- They are primarily nocturnal during the hot summer months and usually dormant during the cold months.

☐ I've seen it!

Longnose Snake

- The body markings of this reptile are highly variable but generally consist of black saddles surrounded by white, cream or yellow spaces.
- Its red or orange irises help distinguish this snake.
- This snake is a constrictor that actively forages for lizards, small mammals, snake and lizard eggs and occasionally grasshoppers.

☐ I've seen it!

Arizona Mud Turtle

- This reptile is diurnal, but becomes more nocturnal during the summer monsoon season.
- They can remain underground for more than a year during prolonged drought conditions.
- Although semi-aquatic, they are able to travel great distances over land in search of water.

 I've seen it!

Campbell Milk Snake

- This reptile occurs mainly in forests and is usually nocturnal.
- There are twenty-four subspecies of this non-venomous snake and it is popular as a pet.
- It is easily confused with the Coral and Mountain King snakes.

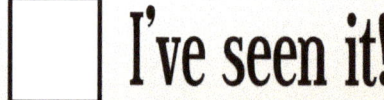 I've seen it!

Gila Monster

- These reptiles are the largest lizards native to the United States.
- They are one of only two venomous lizards in the world.
- They spend around 95 percent of their lives in their homes, which are underground burrows located in rocky foothills.

☐ I've seen it!

ARIZONA
Amphibians & Invertebrates

Colorado River Frog

- This is one of the largest toads found in North America.
- The warts are the toads' defense system as they produce a mild venom.
- They are also known as the "Sonoran Desert Toad".

☐ I've seen it!

Scorpion

- These arachnids are nocturnal hunters.
- There are around 2,000 known species. 80 different species live in the U.S. and 53 species live in Arizona.
- Their sting can be deadly but, not often and they glow under black light.

 I've seen it!

Desert Centipede

- There are two species found in Arizona.
- The "Giant" has an orange body with a black head and tail. The "Common" is tan and brown.
- They inject, or pinch, venom into their prey.

☐ I've seen it!

Tarantula

- These arachnids are very sensitive to vibrations in the ground that may indicate the presence of prey or danger.

- They are equipped with hairs on their abdomen which can be released by kicking with their back legs; the hairs irritate the nose and eyes of would-be attackers.

- They paralyze their prey with venom, then use digestive enzymes to turn their meal into a soupy liquid.

☐ I've seen it!

Black Widow

- In North America, this arachnid is considered the most poisonous one.

- After mating, the female spider usually eats the male.

- Females are usually identified by a red hourglass shape on their abdomen and by their shiny black bodies.

☐ I've seen it!

ARIZONA
CITIES

Glendale

- The city was originally settled in the late 1880s and is part of the Phoenix-Mesa-Scottsdale metropolitan area.
- It is home to the National Football League's (NFL) Arizona Cardinals, the National Hockey League's (NHL) Phoenix Coyotes, and the National Lacrosse League's (NLL) Arizona Sting.
- Population is around 240,000.

☐ Been there!

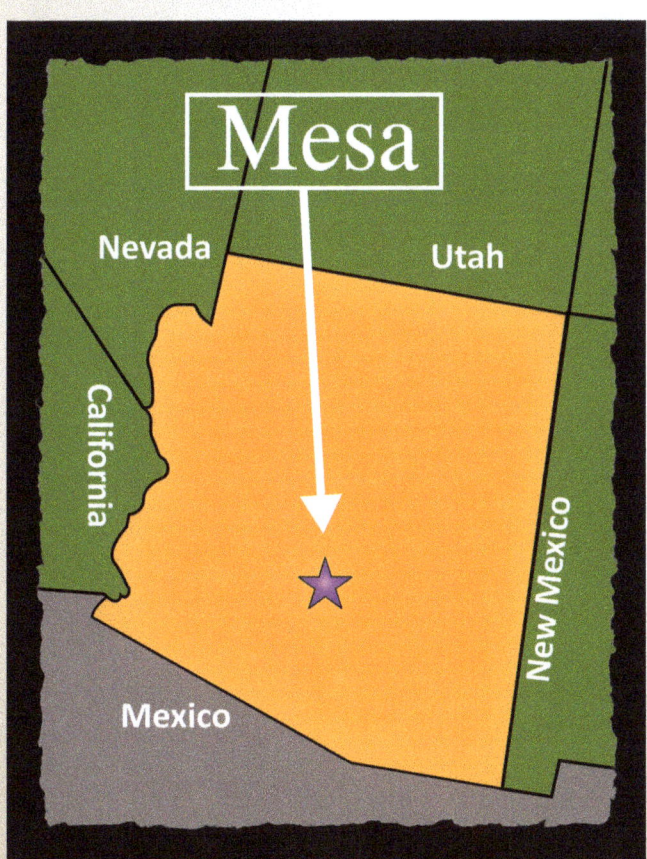

Mesa

- This city's name stems from the Spanish word for "table".
- Prior to being called its current name, the city was known as Zenos.
- It is the 3rd largest city in Arizona and is known as the largest suburban city in the United States.

☐ Been there!

Phoenix

- Around 16 million people visit this metropolitan area every year.
- The world's largest collection of desert plants can be found in this city's Desert Botanical Gardens.
- This is the sixth largest city in the United States.

 Been there!

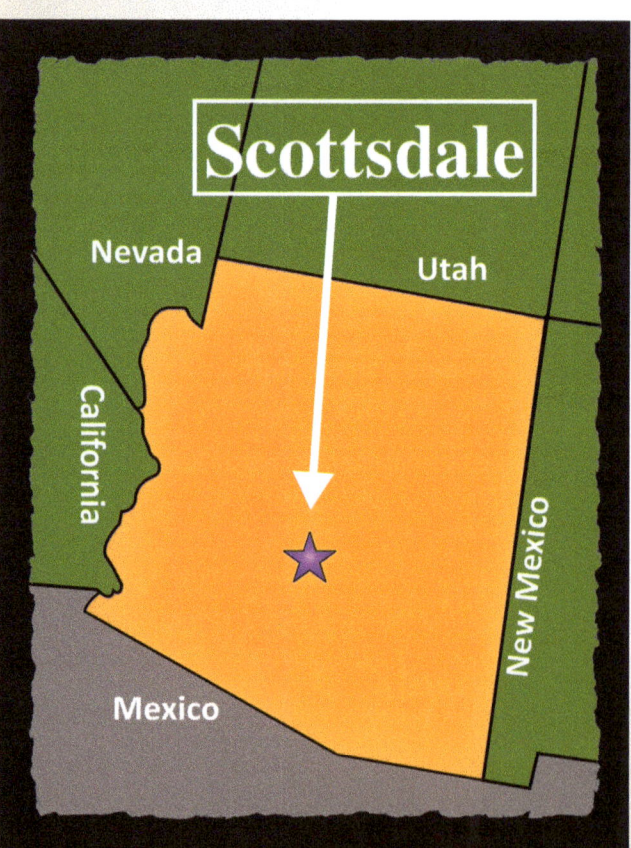

Scottsdale

- This city is home to the Arizona Cowboy College.
- Rather than the usual boring red fire truck, the city went with a more original color: Chartreuse.
- The town was originally named Orangedale, because of all the local citrus groves.

 Been there!

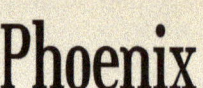

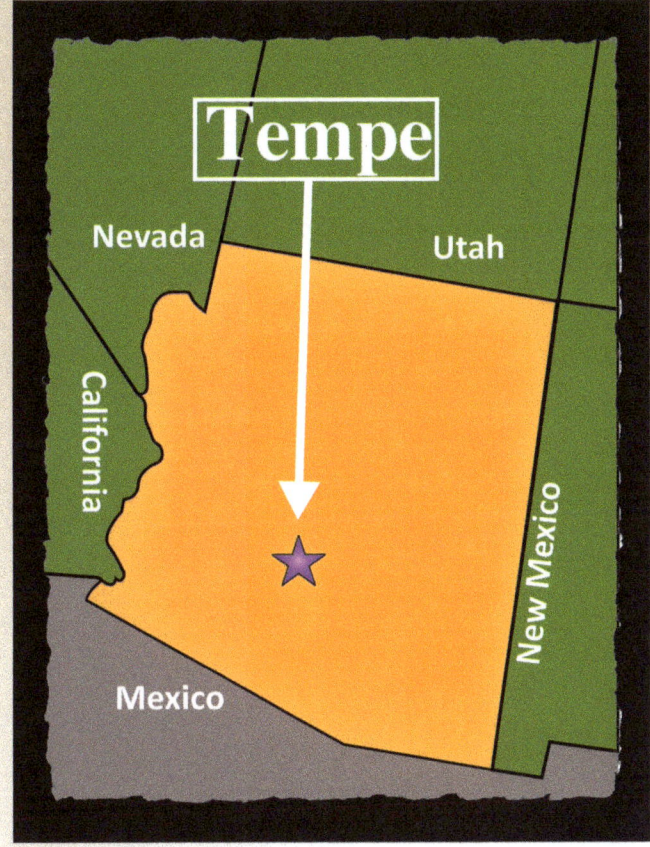

Tempe

- This city was also known as Hayden's Ferry during the territorial times of Arizona.
- Tempe is the location of US Airways Group's corporate headquarters and the home of Arizona State University.
- Tempe is an inner city suburb, located between the core city of Phoenix and the rest of the East Valley.

☐ Been there!

Wickenburg

- This is the oldest town north of Tucson, and the 5th oldest in the state (est. 1863).
- In 1866 it missed becoming the territorial capital by just 2 votes.
- There is a 200 year old mesquite tree located at the corner of US-60 and Tegner Street. The tree served as the town's jail from 1863 to 1890, with outlaws chained to the tree.

☐ Been there!

Flagstaff

- This city is located in the world's largest contiguous Ponderosa Pine forest.
- On average, 100 trains pass through this city each day.
- The city is the county seat for Coconino County, the second largest county in the United States, with an area of 11,896,720 acres.

 Been there!

Showlow

- This is the largest city in the White Mountains and is one of the fastest growing cities in northern Arizona.
- It is said that the city got its name from a card game : "If you can show low, you win".
- The nearby lakes are the only place in the world to find the Apache Trout.

 Been there!

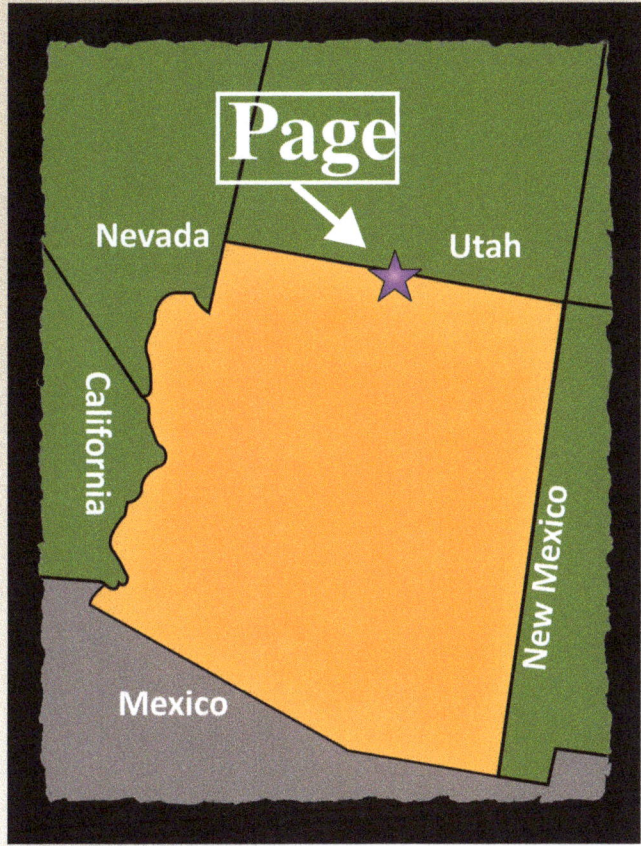

Page

- Unlike other cities in the area, this city was founded in 1957 as a housing community for workers and their families during the construction of nearby Glen Canyon Dam.
- The city is perched atop Manson Mesa at an elevation of 4,300 feet.
- It has become the gateway to the Glen Canyon National Recreation Area and Lake Powell, attracting more than 3 million visitors per year.

☐ Been there!

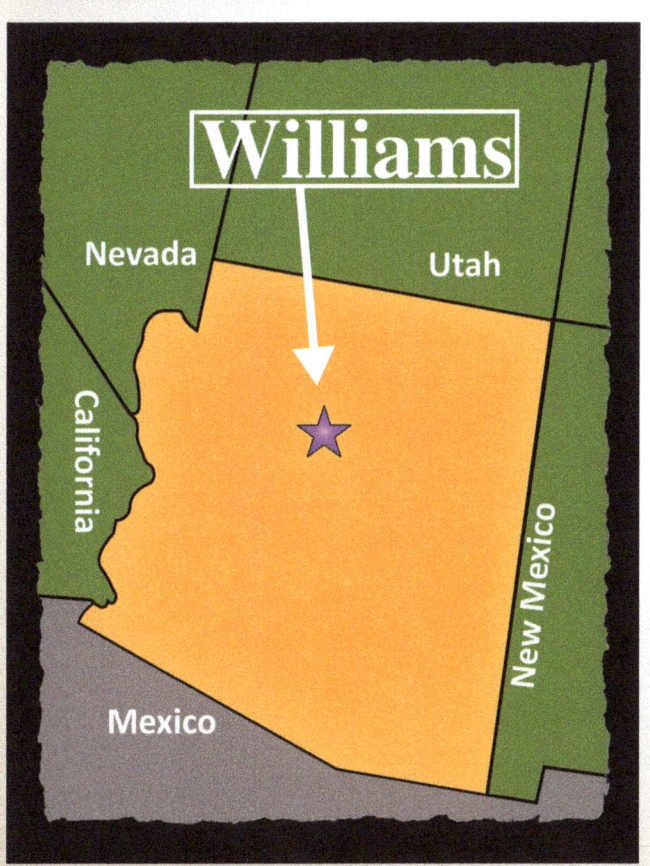

Williams

- This city is west of Flagstaff and is the southern terminus of the Grand Canyon Railway.
- The town, established in 1881 is named after "Old Bill" - a mountain man and trader who often trapped in the area.
- The town was the last town to have its section of Route 66 bypassed.

☐ Been there!

Casa Grande

- This city is approximately halfway between Phoenix and Tucson.
- In September 1880, the community of Terminus was renamed to this current name.
- It was named after the nearby Hohokam people and is Spanish for "big house".

☐ Been there!

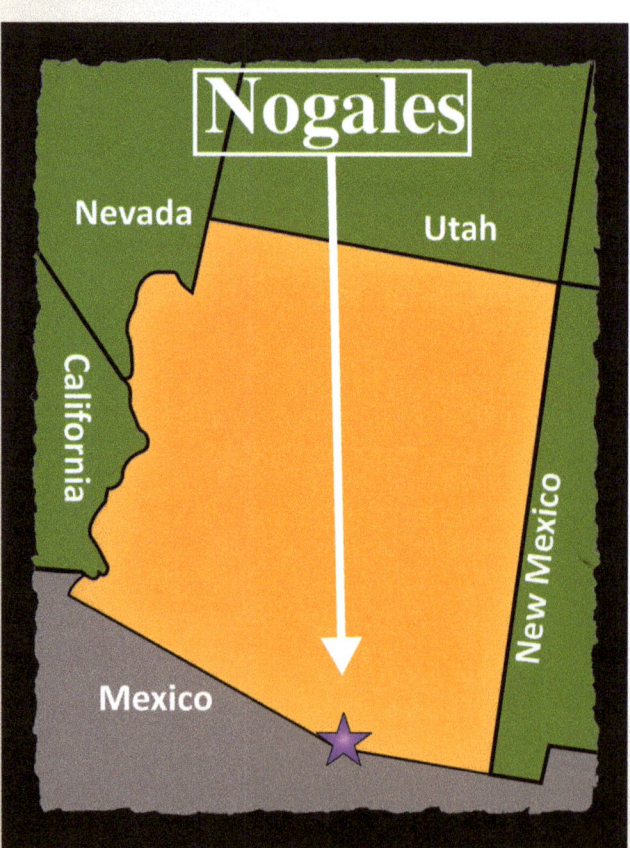

Nogales

- This city is Arizona's largest international border community.
- The city is located at the southern terminus of Interstate 19.
- The city funnels an estimated $30 billion worth of international trade into Arizona and the United States, per year.

☐ Been there!

Winslow

- The historic La Posada Hotel is located here. The hotel was built in 1930 to serve guests using the town's Santa Fe Railway station.
- The Fred Harvey Company owned numerous restaurants and hotels and employed, "Harvey Girls" who were subject to strict rules about their appearances, dress and lifestyles.
- The city achieved national fame in 1972 in the Eagles song "Take it Easy".

☐ Been there!

Benson

- This city was founded in 1880 and served as a rail junction point to obtain ore and refined metal by wagon.
- The city today is perhaps best known as the gateway to Kartchner Caverns State Park.
- In 1936, the Jay Six cattle ranch, which is located just outside of the city, played host to brothers Jack and Joe Kennedy.

☐ Been there!

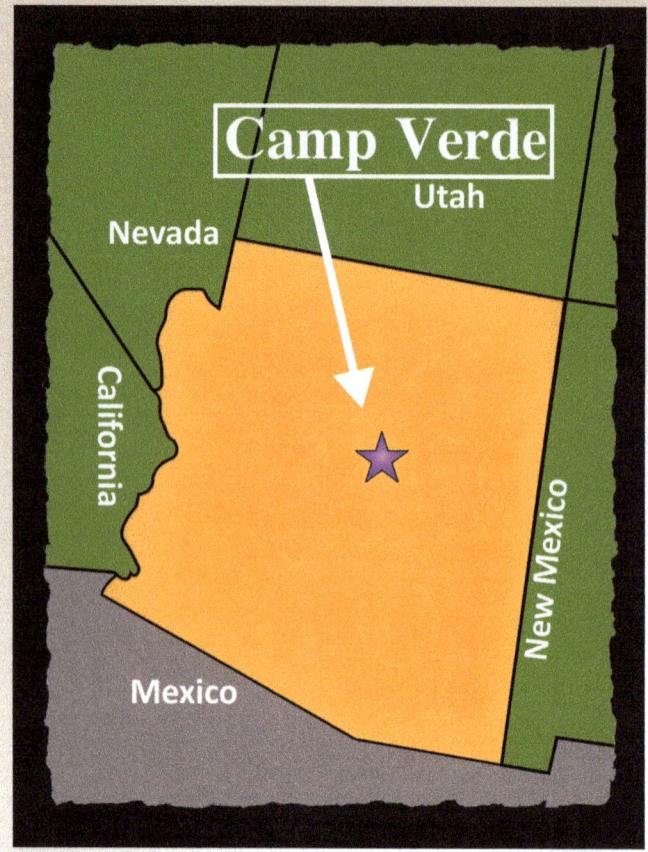

Camp Verde

- The town hosts an annual corn festival in July, sponsored and organized by Hauser and Hauser Farms.
- Montezuma Castle National Monument - a historic five-story American Indian dwelling in a limestone cliff—is located in town.
- Surrounded by the Bradshaw Mountains and Prescott National Forest, the Verde River Valley creates a habitat for bald eagles, hawks, blue heron, beavers and otters.

☐ Been there!

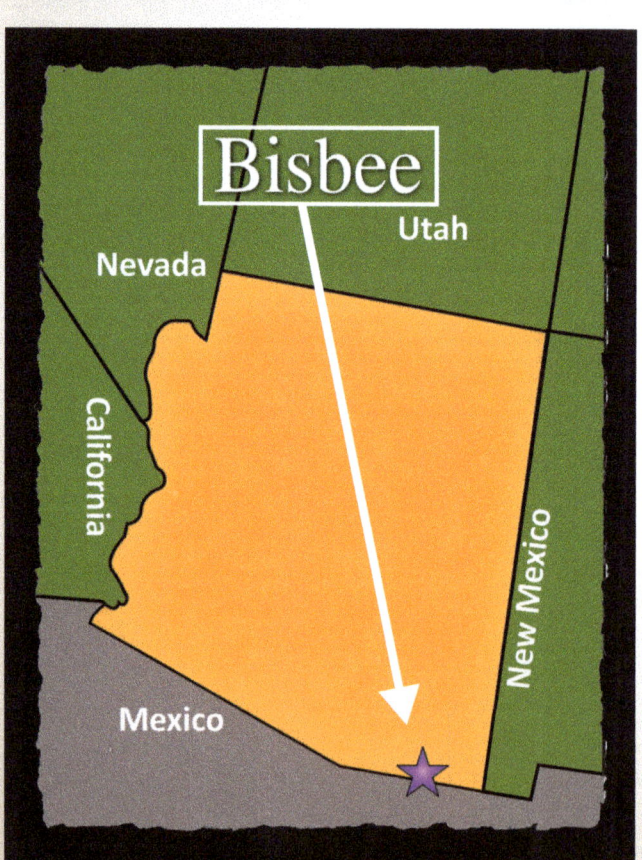

Bisbee

- The city is the county seat of Cochise County.
- It was founded as a copper, gold, and silver mining town in 1880.
- Today, the historic part of the city is home to a thriving downtown cultural scene.

☐ Been there!

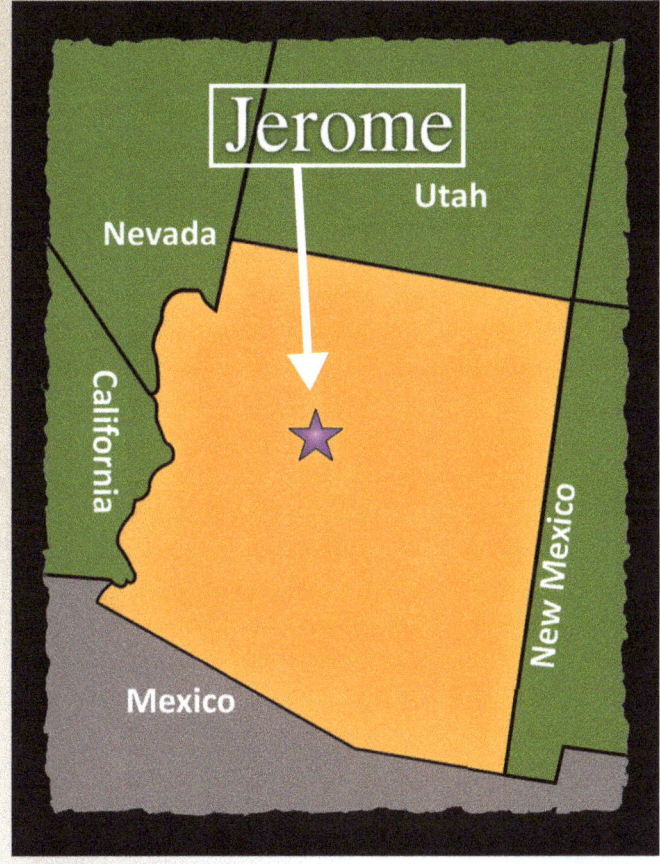

Jerome

- This town is in the Black Hills of Yavapai County and started as a mining camp.
- The main part of the town was leveled four times by the fires of 1894, 1897, 1898 and 1899.
- The city became a National Historic Landmark in 1967.

 Been there!

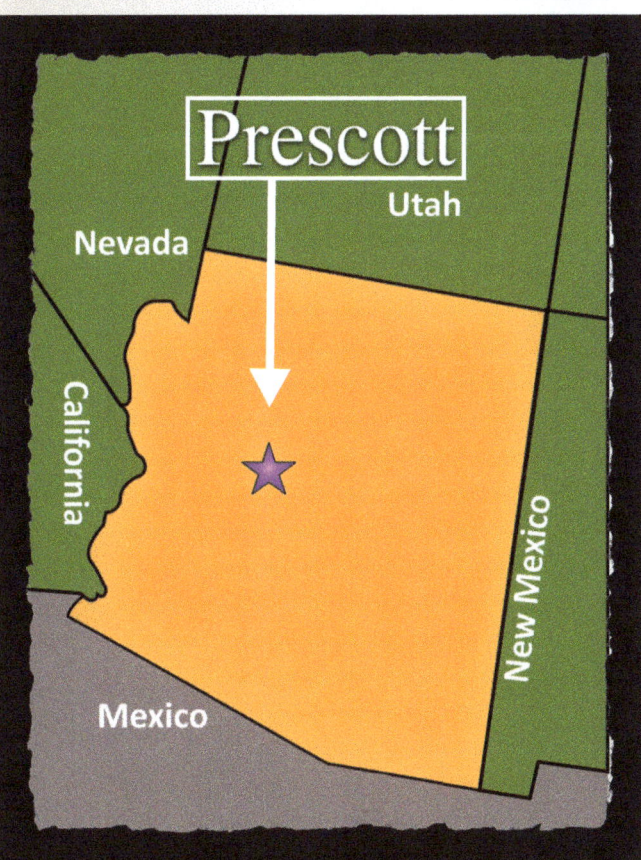

Prescott

- In 1864 the city was designated as the capital of the Arizona Territory, replacing the temporary capital at Fort Whipple. The Territorial Capital was moved to Tucson in 1867. Prescott again became the Territorial Capital in 1877, until Phoenix became the capital in 1889.
- The city has 809 buildings on the National Register of Historic Places.
- The tallest house in North America, Falcon Nest, is located in the city on the slope of Thumb Butte.

☐ Been there!

Sedona

- The city was named after its first Postmaster's wife in early 1900's.
- The famous red color of the surrounding rocks comes from the iron oxide (rust) which have stained the rock formations over a great period of time.
- At an elevation of 4,500 feet, the city has mild winters and hot summers.

☐ Been there!

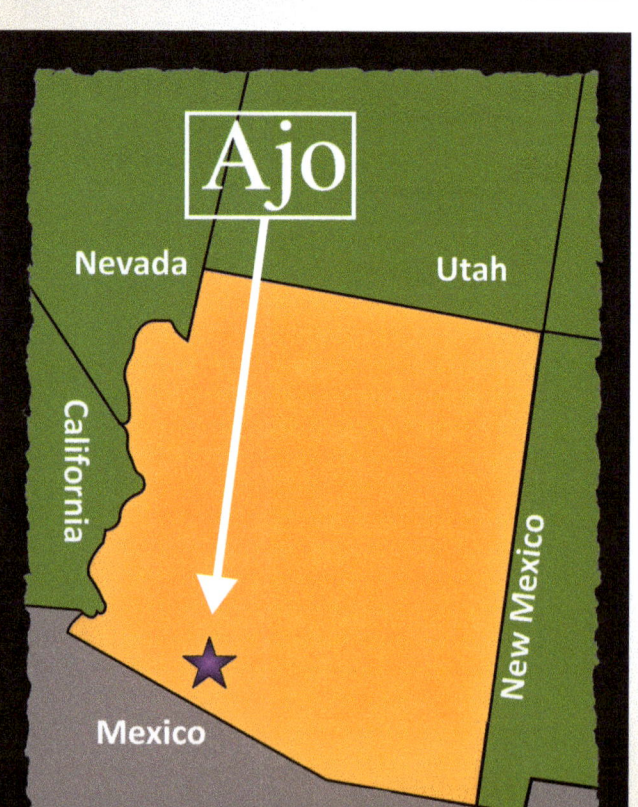

Ajo

- It is the closest community to Organ Pipe Cactus National Monument.
- The city's name is the Spanish word for "garlic".
- High-grade native copper in the area made for the first copper mine in Arizona.

☐ Been there!

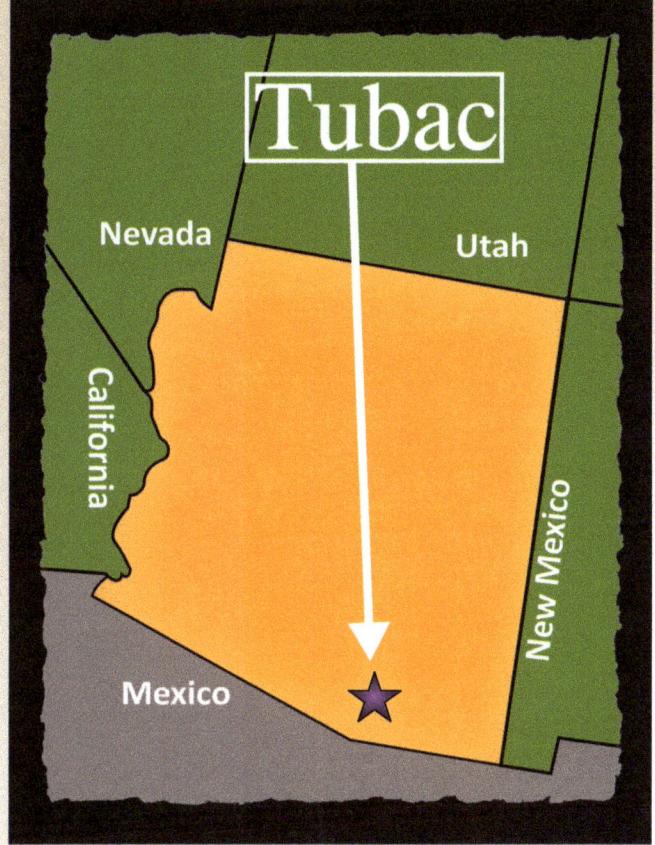

Tubac

- The city name comes from a Hispanic form of the O'odham name, which translates into English as "rotten".
- The remains of the old Spanish presidio are preserved by the city's Presidio State Historic Park.
- During the 19th century, the area was repopulated by miners, farmers and ranchers, but the town is best known today as an artists' colony.

 Been there!

Payson

- The city was founded in 1882 in an area that was known as Green Valley.
- It has been called "The Heart of Arizona".
- The city and area is a popular destination for rock hounds and is known for its rodeo which is the oldest continuous rodeo in the world.

 Been there!

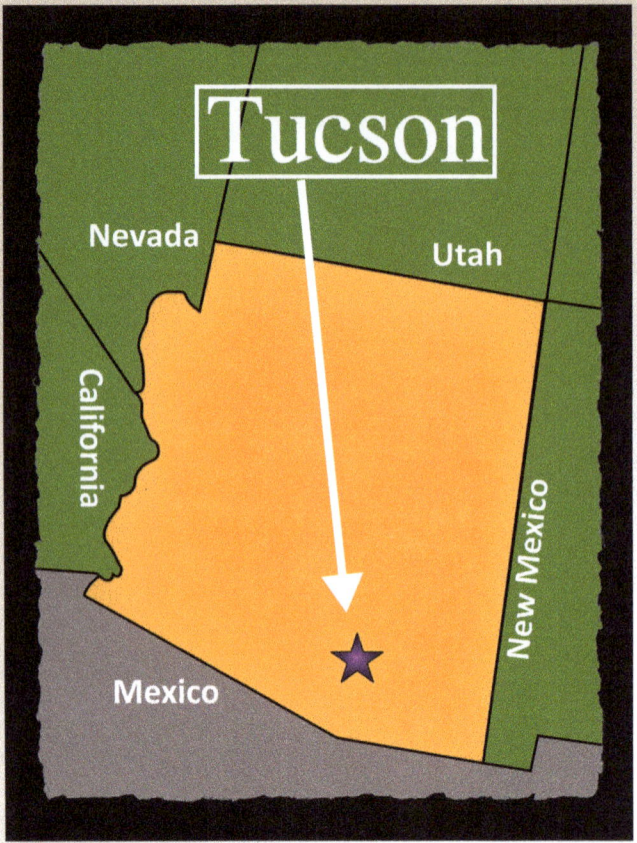

Tucson

- The city is the oldest continuously inhabited settlement in the United States. Natives began farming here nearly 3000 years ago.
- The Rodeo Parade is the largest non-motorized parade in the world.
- Aside from the Amazon Rainforest, the city is home to more bird species than any other region on earth.

☐ Been there!

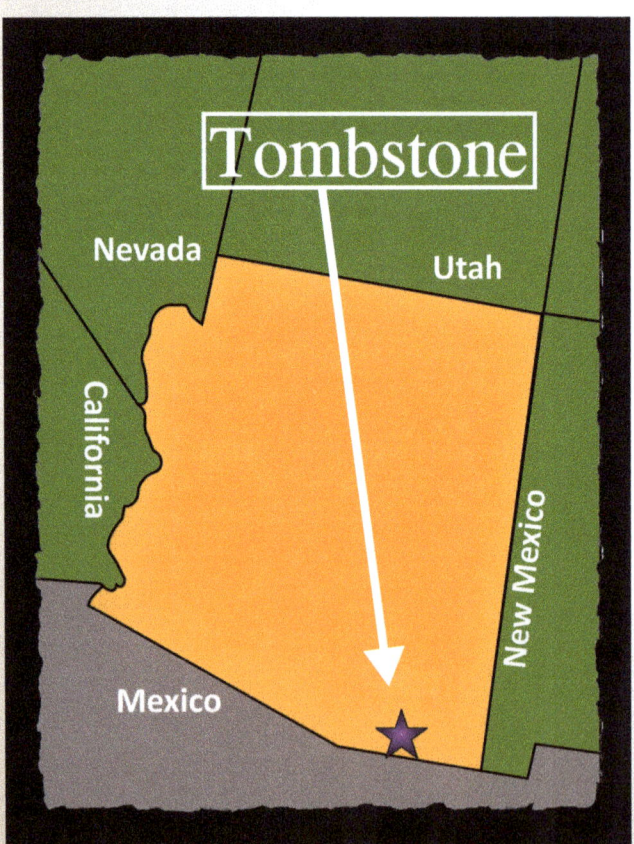

Tombstone

- The town prospered from about 1877 to 1890, and was the largest productive silver district in Arizona.
- The city nearly became a ghost town, saved only because it was the Cochise County seat until 1929.
- It is best known as the site of the Gunfight at the O.K. Corral.

☐ Been there!

Kingman

- Remnants of a wagon road can still be seen in White Cliffs Canyon in this city.
- The city was founded in 1882 when Arizona was still a territory.
- It is situated in the Hualapai Valley between the Cerbat and Hualapai mountain ranges.

 Been there!

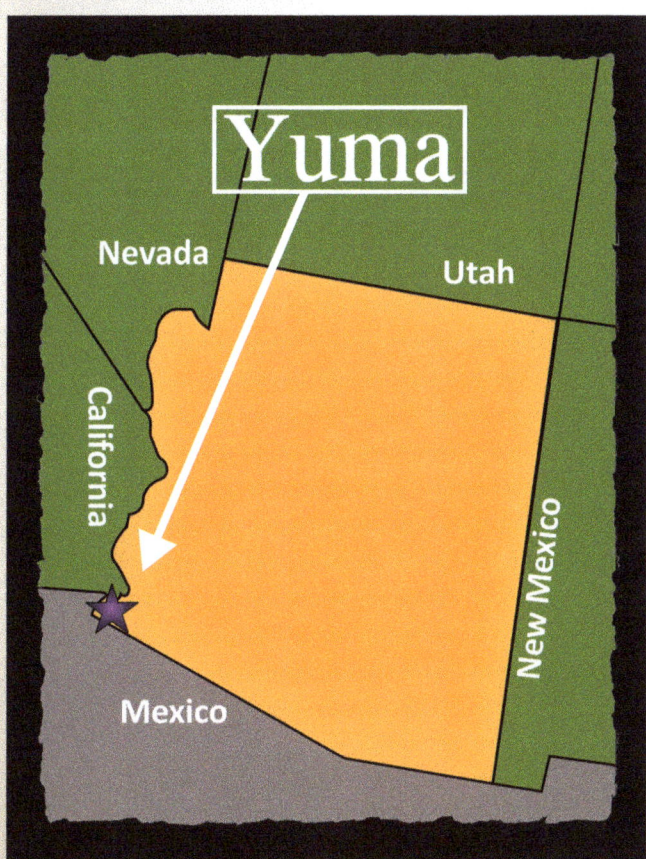

Yuma

- More than 85,000 retirees make this city their winter residence.
- In 1540, Spanish colonial expeditions immediately recognized the natural crossing of the Colorado River as an ideal spot for a city.
- It was known for its ferry crossings for the Southern Emigrant Trail. This was considered the gateway to California.

 Been there!

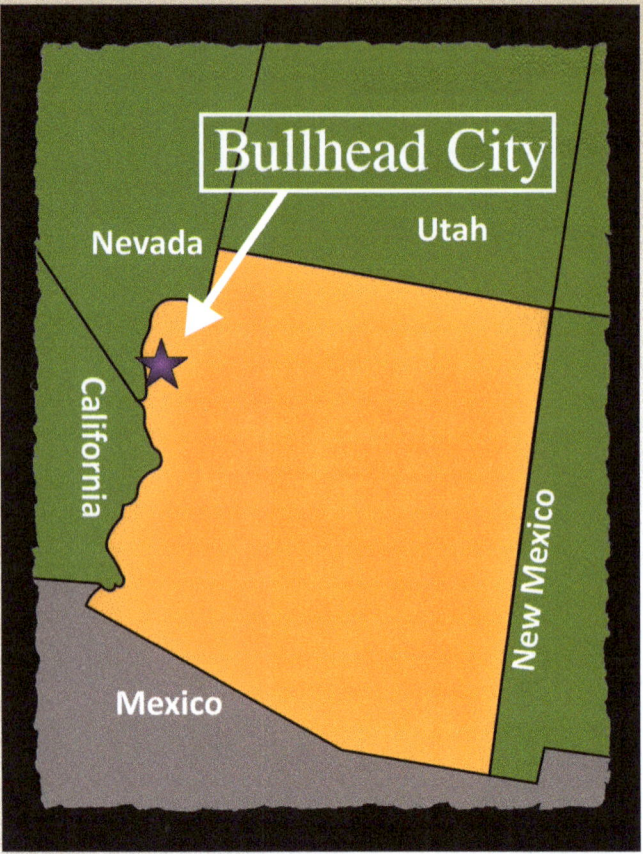

Bullhead City

- The city was founded by William Harrison Hardy in the 1860s, when it was known as Hardyville.
- The city is directly across the Colorado River from Laughlin, Nevada.
- Having been a ghost town since the 1890s, Hardyville would be resurrected with the construction of Davis Dam between 1942 and 1953.

☐ Been there!

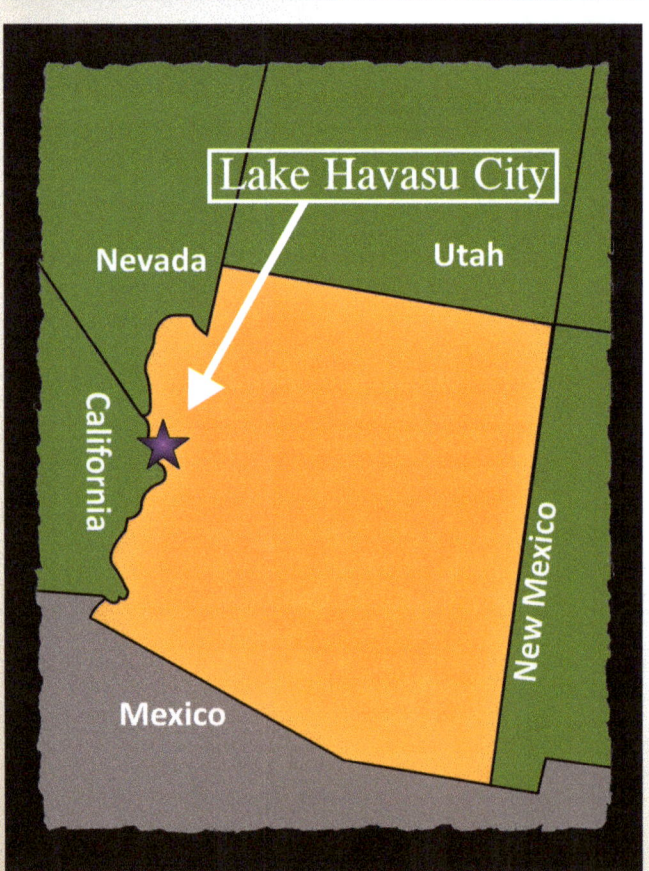

Lake Havasu City

- The community first started as an Army Air Corps rest camp during World War II.
- The city holds the all-time record high temperature in Arizona history with 128°F recorded on June 29, 1994.
- The London Bridge was bought for $2.5 million from the city of London and reconstructed across a narrow channel that leads from Lake Havasu to Thompson Bay.

☐ Been there!

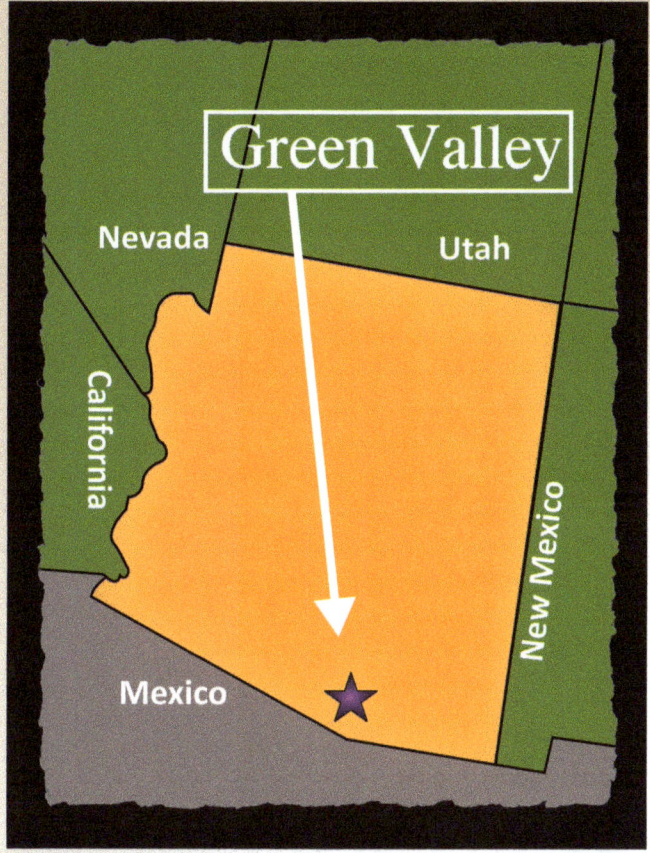

Green Valley

- The "city" is actually a collection of developments and communities located in the extreme southern area of Arizona.
- There are 59 different home owners associations. Most, but not all are age restricted.
- It is surrounded by copper mines and is near the hiking and birding areas of the Santa Rita Mountains.

☐ Been there!

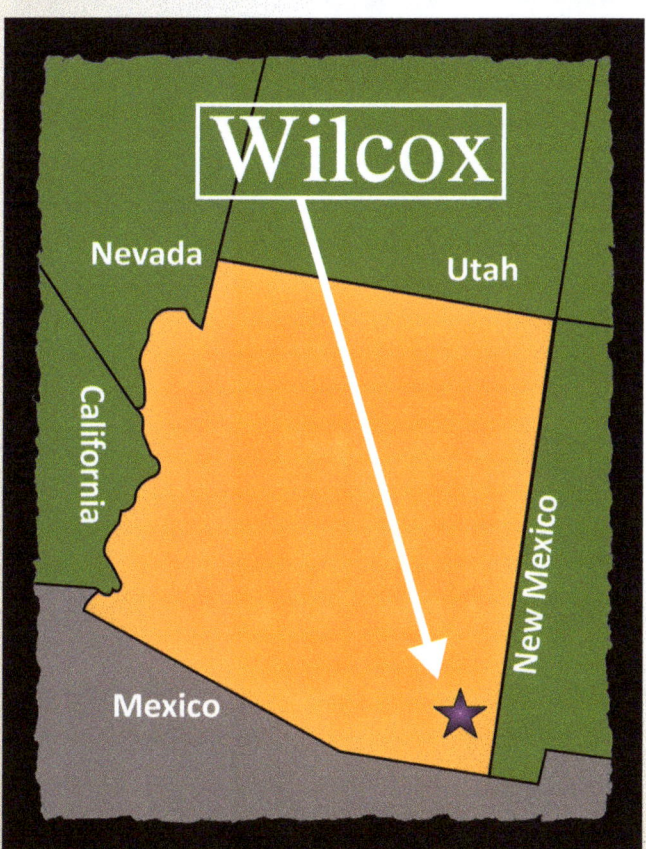

Wilcox

- Originally known as "Maley", the town was founded in 1880 as a whistlestop on the Southern Pacific Railroad.
- The city is home to Arizona's upcoming wine country and produces 74 percent of the wine grapes grown in the state.
- In the early 20th century, the city had the distinction of being a national leader in cattle production.

☐ Been there!

ARIZONA
of INTEREST

University of Arizona

- This campus was founded in 1885, before Arizona was a state.
- At 12 noon everyday the campus clock tower plays, "Bear Down Arizona."
- The Department of Geosciences maintains the #1 mineral database in the world.

☐ Been there!

Arizona State University

- This campus was founded in 1885 as the Arizona Territorial Normal School.
- The university has more than 1,100 clubs.
- Sparky the Sun Devil, the university's mascot since 1946, was created by one-time Disney Studios employee, Bert Anthony.

☐ Been there!

Biosphere 2

- This unique structure, located in Oracle, has 6,500 windows.
- Two missions, between 1991 and 1994, sealed people inside the glass enclosure to measure survivability.
- The University of Arizona took full ownership of the structure in 2011.

☐ **Been there!**

Arizona Snowbowl

- This recreation area is located in the San Francisco Peaks within the Coconino National Forest and not far from Flagstaff.
- Winter visitors can choose from snowshoeing, skiing, cross-country skiing, snowboarding and skijoring.
- The area features a 2,300 ft. vertical drop and a two-mile-long run with an average of 260 inches of snow annually.

☐ **Been there!**

Pima Air & Space Museum

- This is one of the world's largest non-government funded aerospace museums.
- The museum features a display of nearly 300 aircraft spread out over 80 acres on a campus occupying 127 acres.
- Since 1991, it has also been the home to the Arizona Aviation Hall of Fame.

☐ Been there!

Desert Botanical Garden

- The 140 acre garden is located in Papago Park in Phoenix.
- The garden has more than 50,000 desert plants on display.
- It was founded by the Arizona Cactus and Native Flora Society in 1937 and officially established at this site in 1939.

☐ Been there!

Mt. Lemmon Ski Valley

- This is the southernmost ski destination in the continental United States.
- It is part of the Coronado National Forest and is located near the mountaintop village of Summerhaven.
- The ski lift runs year round, as a "Sky Ride" experience in the summertime offering wonderful views.

 Been there!

Grand Canyon University

- This college was established as a Baptist-affiliated institution with an emphasis on religious studies.
- The college was chartered in 1949, with 16 faculty and approximately 100 students, in the city of Prescott.
- In 1951, the college relocated to a 90 acre tract in West Phoenix and was fully accredited in 1968.

 Been there!

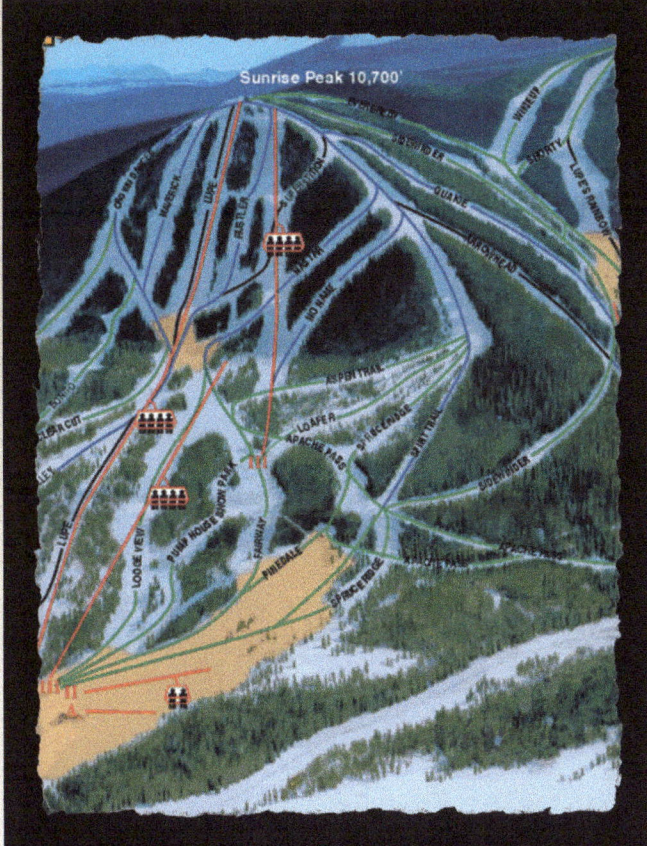

Sunrise Ski

- This ski resort is located near Greer, Arizona.
- The resort is situated on the Colorado Plateau of the White Mountains and consists of three mountains named Sunrise Peak, Cyclone Peak, and Apache Peak.
- It is owned and operated by the White Mountain Apache Tribe.

☐ Been there!

Northern Arizona University

- This university is a 4 year public research institution in Flagstaff and a designated Hispanic-serving institution.
- It is home to nine colleges granting bachelor's degrees in 12 academic divisions.
- This school was established in 1899 and is one of the 3 colleges located in Flagstaff, Arizona.

☐ Been there!

Old Tucson Studios

- This is an American movie studio and theme park located adjacent to the Tucson mountains.
- It was built in 1939 for the movie *Arizona*.
- It had been used for the filming of many movies and television westerns. It then opened to the public in 1960.

☐ Been there!

Arizona State Capitol

- The copper in the dome of the original building is the equivalent of nearly 5 million pennies.
- The original building is now home to the Arizona Capital Museum.
- The building is listed on the National Register of Historic Places.

☐ Been there!

Phoenix Zoo

- This operates on 125 acres of land in the Papago Park area of Phoenix.
- It has over 1,400 animals on display and contains 2.5 miles of walking trails.
- It opened in 1962 and is the largest privately owned, non-profit in the United States.

☐ Been there!

Herd Museum

- It was founded, in 1929, as a small museum in a small southwestern town.
- The museum experienced a significant expansion in 1983, when it nearly doubled in size to 78,000 sq. ft., then added 50,000 sq. ft. in 1999.
- It is now recognized internationally for the quality of its collections, world-class exhibitions, educational programming and its unmatched festivals.

☐ Been there!

Roosevelt Row Phoenix

- This is a walkable arts district in downtown Phoenix.
- It serves as a central hub for art and culture in the downtown Phoenix area.
- The flower shop, at Fifth Street and Roosevelt, has been in continuous operation since 1948.

☐ Been there!

Phoenix Art Museum

- A community center since 1959, it hosts year-round programs of festivals, live performances, independent art films and educational programs.
- It also features The Hub - an interactive space for children.
- It displays international exhibitions alongside its comprehensive collection of more than 18,000 pieces of art.

☐ Been there!

University of Phoenix Stadium

- This stadium has the first fully retractable playing field in North America.

- The stadium's retractable roof takes around 15 minutes to open and close.

- The stadium has 63,400 permanent seats but can expand to up to 72,200 for larger events, like the Super Bowl.

 Been there!

Sea Life Aquarium

- This aquarium features more than 30 display tanks in 12 distinct habitats housing more than 5,000 creatures in 200,000 gallons of water.

- Located Tempe, it cost $15 million to build the 26,000 square foot aquarium.

- It is owned by Merlin Entertainment which also owns and operates Lego Land in San Diego and Sea Life in Carlsbad, California.

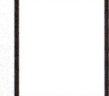 Been there!

Haboob / Dust Storm

- This is a dust storm that forms in the downdrafts of a thunderstorm.
- When the wind hits the Earth, it starts to move sideways and picks up dirt and dust.
- In Arizona, the most common term for this event is either "dust storm" or "sandstorm".

☐ Been there!

Monsoon

- By definition, this word refers to a season. To say "monsoon season" is redundant.
- Arizona receives 32 percent of its yearly rain totals during this time.
- Lightning will strike, on average, about 500,000 times during this season.

☐ Been there!

Mexican Border Wall

- This section of Arizona is approximately 370 miles long.

- More construction along this corridor could negatively impact 23 endangered and at-risk species, including the Sonoran pronghorn antelope.

- Along the Arizona western desert, the government has waived 41 federal environmental laws to expedite construction.

 Been there!

Hoover Dam

- It was originally recommended the dam be constructed at Boulder Canyon but was, instead, constructed at Black Canyon.

- An entire city was created for people working on the dam.

- The dam created America's largest reservoir, Lake Mead

 Been there!

Desert Museum

- The Museum was founded in 1952 and is dedicated to the interpretation of the Sonoran Desert region.
- 85% of the museum is outdoors.
- There are two miles of walking paths, 16 individual gardens, 1,200 native plant species, 56,000 individual plants and 230 native animals.

☐ Been there!

Navajo Bridge

- These two bridges, one historic and one new, represent one of only seven land crossings of the Colorado River for 750 miles.
- The bridge was opened to traffic in 1929.
- When it opened, it was the highest steel arch bridge in the world and made traveling between Utah and Arizona much easier.

☐ Been there!

Casa Grande Ruins

- Archaeologists have no clue what this structure's actual purpose was.
- The site was designated a National Monument in 1918.
- The ruins of a walled compound were discovered in 1694 by a Jesuit missionary.

☐ Been there!

Golf Courses

- There are over 300 courses throughout Arizona.
- Roughly 20,000 jobs are created in Arizona each year as a result of this industry.
- In 1900, on the corner of Third Street and Roosevelt in central Phoenix, a dusty nine-hole dirt course became the first established course in Arizona.

☐ Been there!

Vermilion Cliffs

- These cliffs are made up of deposited silt and desert dunes, cemented by infiltrated carbonates and intensely colored by red iron oxide and other minerals, particularly bluish manganese.

- The cliffs were located along an important route from Utah to Arizona that was used by settlers during the 19th Century.

- The region was designated a National Monument in 2000 by president Bill Clinton.

☐ Been there!

Hole in the Rock - Papago Park

- This is a series of openings eroded in a small hill composed of bare red sandstone.

- The formation is a popular attraction in Papago Park.

- There is evidence that the Hohokam tribe used and recorded the position of sunlight shining through the openings.

☐ Been there!

Glen Canyon Dam & Bridge

- At the time of its completion in 1959, this bridge was the highest arch bridge in the world and the second highest bridge of any type.

- This 710-foot high dam was completed in 1966 and formed Lake Powell - one of the largest man-made reservoirs in the U.S.

- The dam has been criticized for the large evaporative losses from Lake Powell and its impact on the ecology of the Grand Canyon.

☐ Been there!

Spider Rock Canyon de Chelly

- This National Monument, located in northeastern Arizona within the boundaries of the Navajo Nation, was established on April 1, 1931.

- The park's distinctive geologic feature is a sandstone spire that rises 750 feet from the canyon floor.

- It's named for Spider Woman, a key figure in Navajo lore.

☐ Been there!

Papago Ponds

- There are 3 bodies of water that make up this natural feature.
- The first pond covers 1 acre, max depth 8 ft. - the second pond covers 2 acres, max depth 7 ft. and the third pond covers 3 acres, max depth 11 ft.
- They are home to channel catfish, rainbow trout, largemouth bass, bluegill, red dear sunfish, crappie, tilapia, and carp, stocked by the Arizona Game and Fish Department.

☐ Been there!

El Capitan Peak

- This is a peak south of Monument Valley, Arizona, which rises over 1500 feet above the surrounding terrain.
- It is an eroded volcanic plug consisting of volcanic breccia.
- It is also known as Agathla Peak.

☐ Been there!

Mission San Xavier del Bak

- This National Historic Landmark was founded as a Catholic mission by Father Eusebio Kino in 1692.
- Construction of the current church began in 1783 and was completed in 1797.
- This is the oldest intact European structure in Arizona and is widely considered to be the finest example of Spanish Colonial architecture in the United States.

☐ Been there!

Sabino Canyon

- This is a significant canyon located in the Santa Catalina Mountains.
- It is a popular recreation area for residents and visitors of Southern Arizona, providing a place to walk, hike or ride.
- The Emergency Relief Agency built Sabino Dam and nine bridges over Sabino Creek in an attempt to build a road to the top of Mount Lemmon. The road travels about 4.5 miles into the canyon, but was not completed.

☐ Been there!

Mt. Lemmon

- This mountain has a summit elevation of 9,159 feet.
- It is the highest point in the Santa Catalina Mountains and is located in the Coronado National Forest.
- Atop the peak is an observatory run by the University of Arizona.

☐ Been there!

Walnut Canyon

- This National Monument is located about 10 miles southeast of downtown Flagstaff, Arizona.
- The canyon was proclaimed a National Monument on November 30, 1915 by President Woodrow Wilson to preserve the ancient cliff dwellings.
- A long loop trail descends 185 ft. into the canyon, passing 25 cliff dwelling rooms constructed by the Sinagua, a pre-Columbian cultural group.

☐ Been there!

Wupatki National Monument

- This National Monument is located near Flagstaff and is rich in Native American ruins.
- On October 15, 1966, it was listed on the National Register of Historic Places. The listing included 3 buildings and 29 structures on 35,253 acres.
- This site also contains a geological blowhole where wind escapes from a cave system.

☐ Been there!

Painted Desert

- This area was named by an expedition under Francisco Vazquez de Coronado on his 1540 quest to find the Seven Cities of Cibola.
- Much of the area lies within Petrified Forest National Park.
- The area is known for its brilliant and varied colors, that not only include the more common red rock, but also shades of lavender.

☐ Been there!

Kartchner Caves

- These caverns are home to the world's longest soda straw stalactites.
- The cave was discovered in 1984 by Gary Tenen and Randy Tufts, but they didn't tell owners James and Lois Kartchner about it until 1988.
- The public finally learned of the cave in 1988 when it became an Arizona State Park.

 Been there!

Yuma Prison Historical

- This territorial prison is a living museum of the Old West.
- More than 3,000 desperadoes were imprisoned in rock and adobe cells here during 1876 through 1909.
- By 1907, the prison was severely overcrowded, and there was no room on Prison Hill for expansion. Convicts constructed a new facility in Florence, Arizona.

 Been there!

Humphreys Peak

- This is Arizona's highest mountain and the highest point of the San Francisco Peaks.
- It is the 26th most prominent mountain in the lower 48 states with an elevation of 12,637.
- Native Americans are believed to have made the first ascent of this mountain.

 ☐ Been there!

Cathedral Rock - Sedona

- This is a natural sandstone butte on the Sedona skyline and one of the most photographed sights in Arizona.
- The summit elevation is 4,967 ft.
- It was called "Court House Rock" on some early maps.

☐ Been there!

Saguaro National Park

- This National Park is a 91,442 acre park located in southern Arizona.
- It is divided into two districts - Tucson Mountain District (west) and the Rincon Mountain District (east).
- The saguaro cactus can only be found in the Sonoran Desert. This National Park protects portions of this 100,000 square mile desert.

☐ Been there!

Toroweap Point - Grand Canyon

- This is a viewpoint within the Grand Canyon National Park.
- The overlook is the only viewpoint in the National Park from where the Colorado River can be seen vertically below.
- The name, a Paiute term meaning "dry or barren valley", strictly refers to the valley and the overlook.

☐ Been there!

The Arizona Wave - Coyote Buttes

- This unusual sandstone rock formation looks more like a surrealist painting than an actual place.

- It is a sandstone rock formation in the Coyote Buttes near the Arizona-Utah border.

- It is considered one of the most photographed landscapes in the United States yet, only 20 hikers a day are allowed to visit.

☐ Been there!

Organ Pipe Cactus National Monument

- This National Monument is the only place in the United States to see large stands of this type of cactus.

- This National Monument is 517 square miles in size.

- In 1976 the Monument was declared a Biosphere Reserve by UNESCO, and in 1977 95% of the land was declared a wilderness area.

☐ Been there!

Barringer Meteor Crater

- This is a meteorite impact crater located in the northern Arizona desert.
- The site was formerly known as the Canyon Diablo Crater.
- The crater is privately owned by the Barringer family through their Barringer Crater Company, which proclaims it to be the "best preserved meteorite crater on Earth".

 Been there!

Montezuma's Castle

- This National Monument is an archaeological site in central Arizona.
- The monument lies in the Verde River valley just northeast of Camp Verde.
- Established in 1906, it has an area of 1.3 square miles and comprises one of the best preserved pre-Columbian Pueblo Indian cliff dwellings in the United States.

 Been there!

Lake Powell

- This lake has over 2,000 miles of shoreline which is more than the combined states on the Pacific Coast.
- It is 400 feet deep and 186 miles long.
- The lake was formed when the Glen Canyon Dam was completed in 1963. It took 17 years to reach "full pool".

☐ Been there!

Havasupai (Havasu) Falls

- To access this area, you begin on the Hualapai Indian Reservation.
- The name translates to "people of the blue-green waters".
- The creek is fed by a natural spring so it is not prone to drying up like other creeks around Arizona.

☐ Been there!

Superstition Mountain(s)

- This is a large mountain that is a popular recreation destination for residents of the Phoenix, Arizona area.
- It is part of a range that has the same name.
- The legend of the Lost Dutchman's Gold Mine centers around these mountains.

 Been there!

Tumacacori Nation Historic Park

- This National Historic Park is located in the upper Santa Cruz River Valley in southern Arizona.
- The park protects the ruins of three Spanish mission communities, two of which are National Historic Landmark sites.
- It also contains the landmark 1937 Museum building, also a National Historic Landmark.

 Been there!

Horsehoe Bend

- This bend in the Colorado River is located near the town of Page, Arizona.
- This feature is located 5 miles downstream from the Glen Canyon Dam and Lake Powell.
- The view point/lookout is 1,000 ft. above the river.

 Been there!

Petrified Forest National Park

- The area was first protected as a National Monument in 1906. The park was elevated to National Park status in 1962.
- The park protects one of the largest concentrations of petrified wood in the world.
- It is the only National Park that closes at night.

☐ Been there!

Tohono Chul Park

- This park contains 49 acres of thematic botanical gardens.
- The name translates to "desert corner".
- Richard and Jean Wilson are credited with founding this park that was formally dedicated in 1985.

☐ Been there!

Kitt Peak Observatory

- This point of interest is located in the Quinlan Mountains and is 55 miles west-southwest of Tucson.
- It is home to 22 optical and 2 radio telescopes - the largest collection of telescopes in the northern hemisphere.
- It is home to the McMath-Pierce Solar Telescope which is currently the largest solar telescope in the world.

☐ Been there!

Other things I have seen in Arizona!

	I've seen it!
	I've seen it!
	I've seen it!
	I've seen it!
	I've seen it!
	I've seen it!
	I've seen it!
	I've seen it!
	I've seen it!

Other things I have seen in Arizona!

	I've seen it!
	I've seen it!
	I've seen it!
	I've seen it!
	I've seen it!
	I've seen it!
	I've seen it!
	I've seen it!
	I've seen it!

Try our other Learning, Thinking & Children's Books!
Visit : MissingPiecePress.com

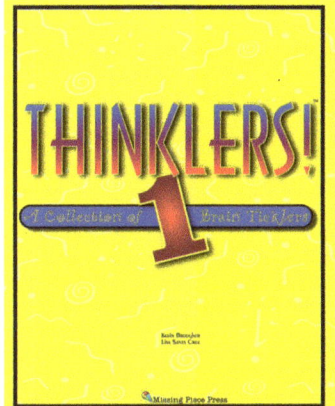
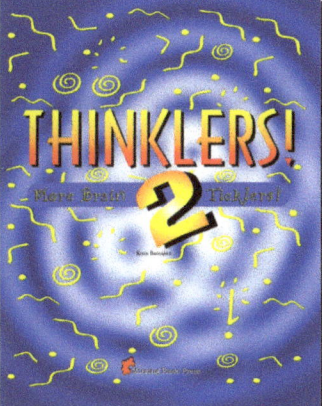
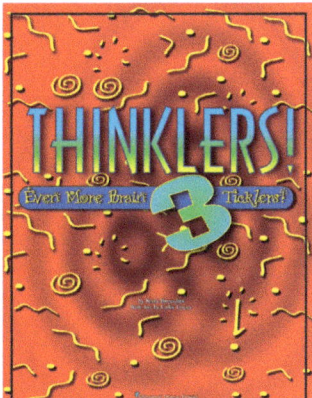

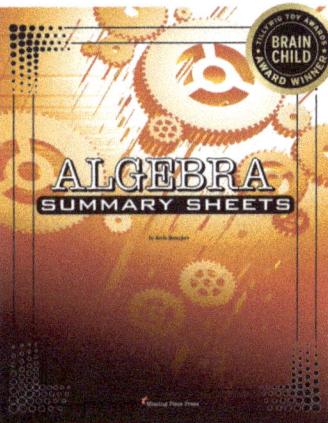

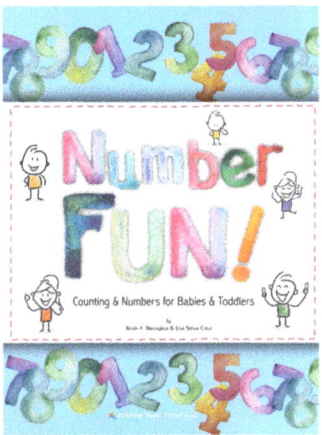

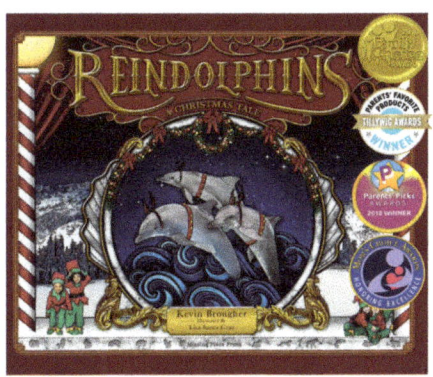

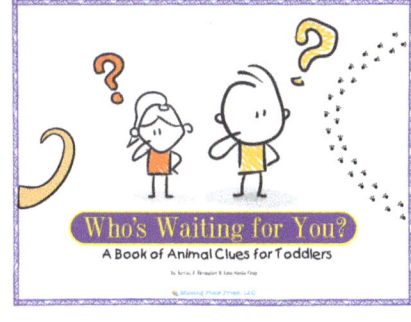

Try our other award-winning games!
Visit : MissingPiecePress.com

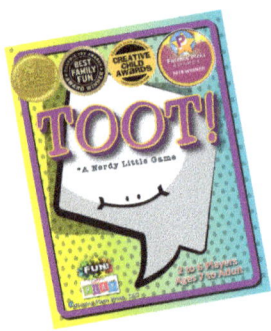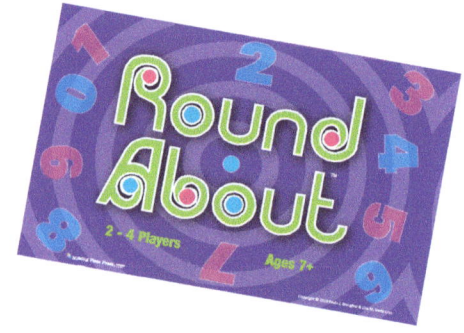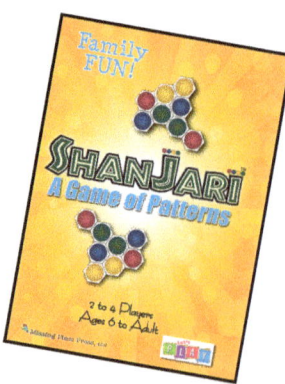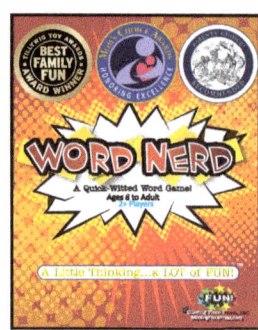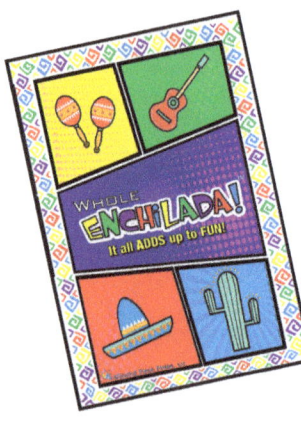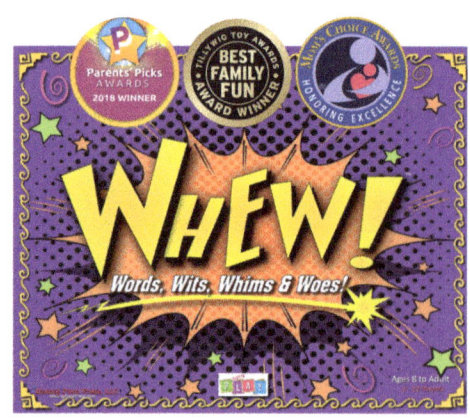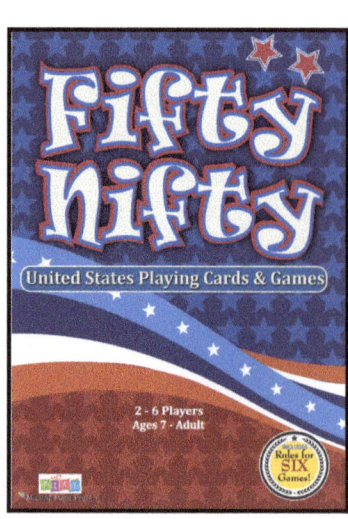

Missing Piece Press, LLC

Copyright © 2019 Kevin J. Brougher & Lisa M. Santa Cruz